The Planet Promise
I promise to:

Rethink what I use and buy.
Refuse what I don't need.
Reduce my waste and carbon footprint.
Reuse things when I can.
Recycle as much as I can.
Rot food in a <u>compost bin</u>.
Repair broken things.

Earth's Eco-Warriors are going green for good! But what does it mean to 'go green'? Earth has a certain amount of <u>natural resources</u> that we use to do almost everything. 'Going green' means living in a <u>sustainable</u> way that helps look after Earth's natural resources and the <u>environment</u>. We need to think about how we can reduce our carbon footprints to help the environment.

BookLife PUBLISHING

©2020 BookLife Publishing Ltd.
King's Lynn
Norfolk PE30 4LS

Written by: Shalini Vallepur
Edited by: Emilie Dufresne
Designed by: Gareth Liddington

All rights reserved. Printed in Malaysia.

A catalogue record for this book is available from the British Library.

ISBN: 978-1-83927-061-1

Eco-words that look like <u>this</u> are explained on page 24.

WE ARE EARTH'S ECO-WARRIORS

Are you an Eco-Warrior? Greta, Bailey and Pietro are Earth's Eco-Warriors! Eco-Warriors care about the environment and planet Earth. They made the Planet Promise and are trying to save planet Earth.

GRETA BAILEY PIETRO ROCKY

"Join us, Earth's Eco-Warriors, as we go green for good!"

The summer holidays had just started and Earth's Eco-Warriors were ready to go on a summer adventure. There was just one problem – they didn't know where to go!

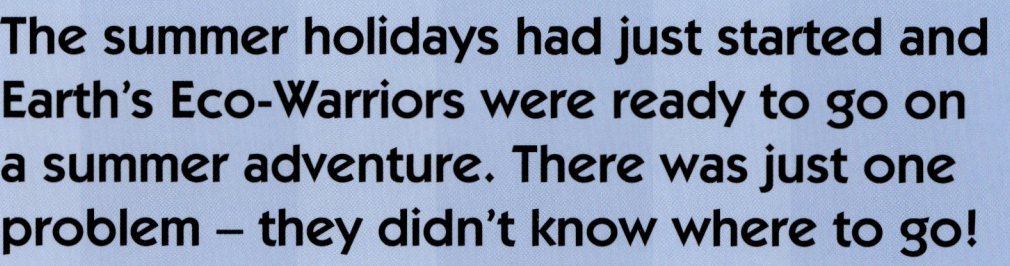

I think we should go to Spain.

I say we fly to Australia!

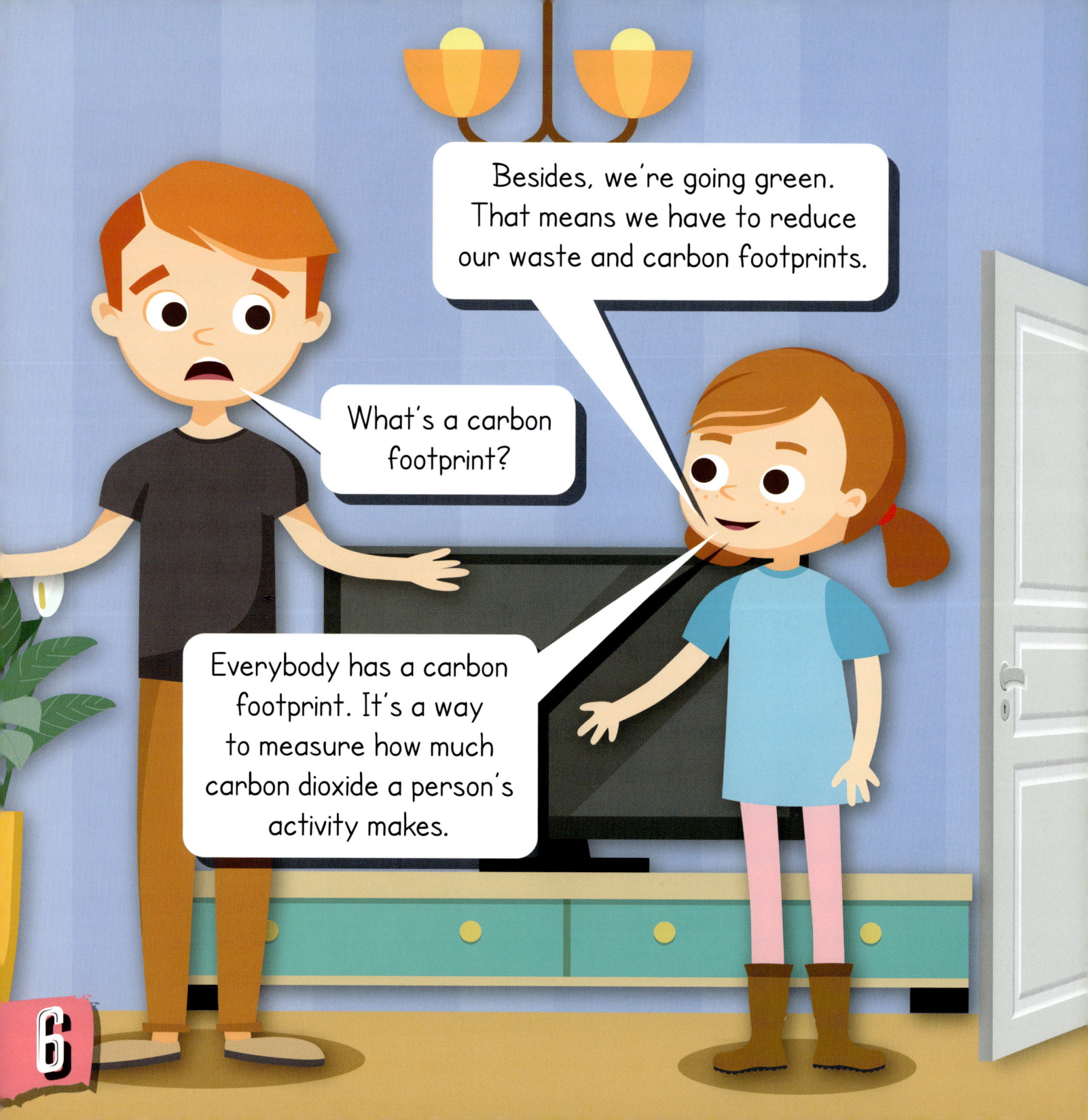

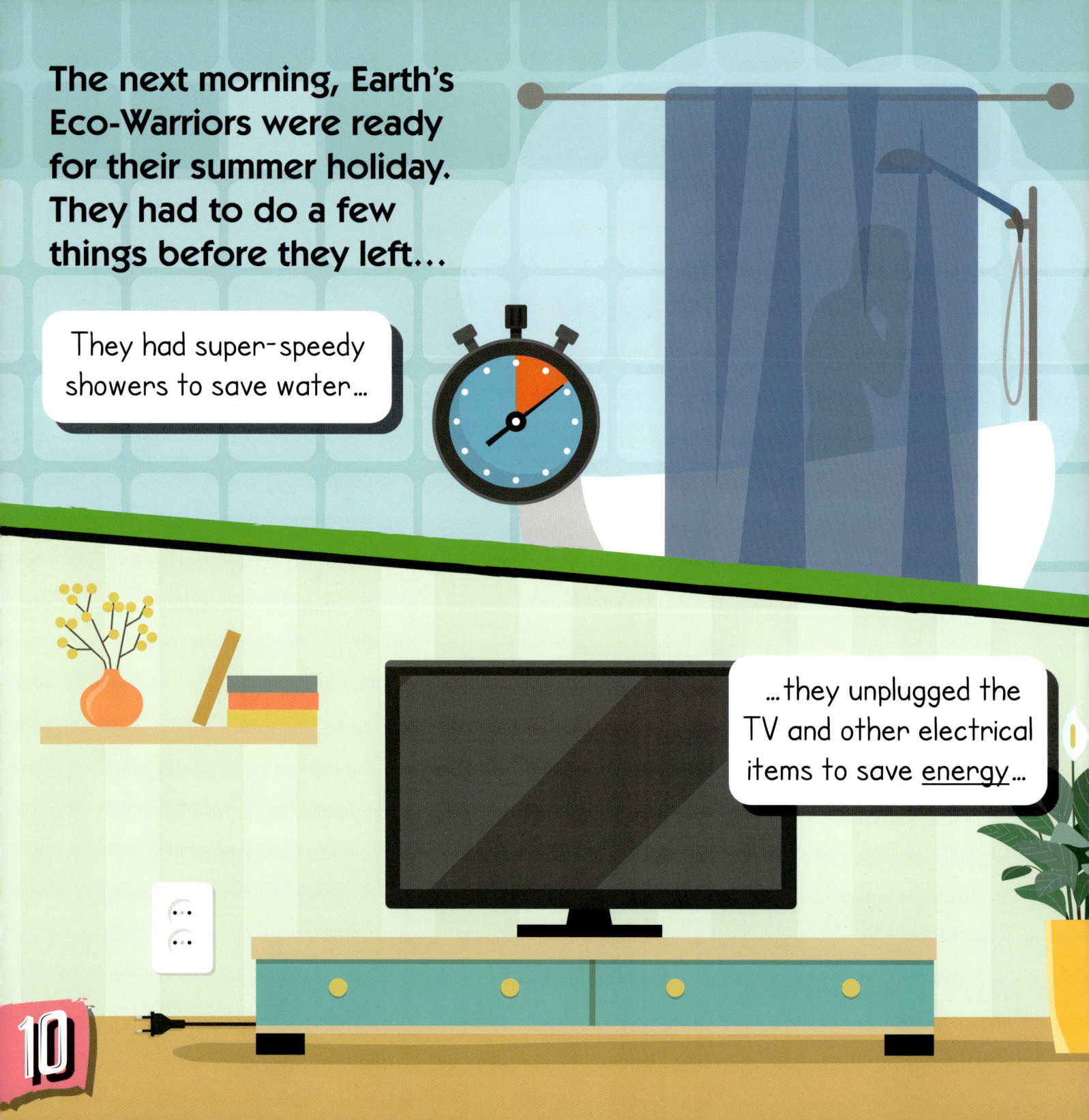

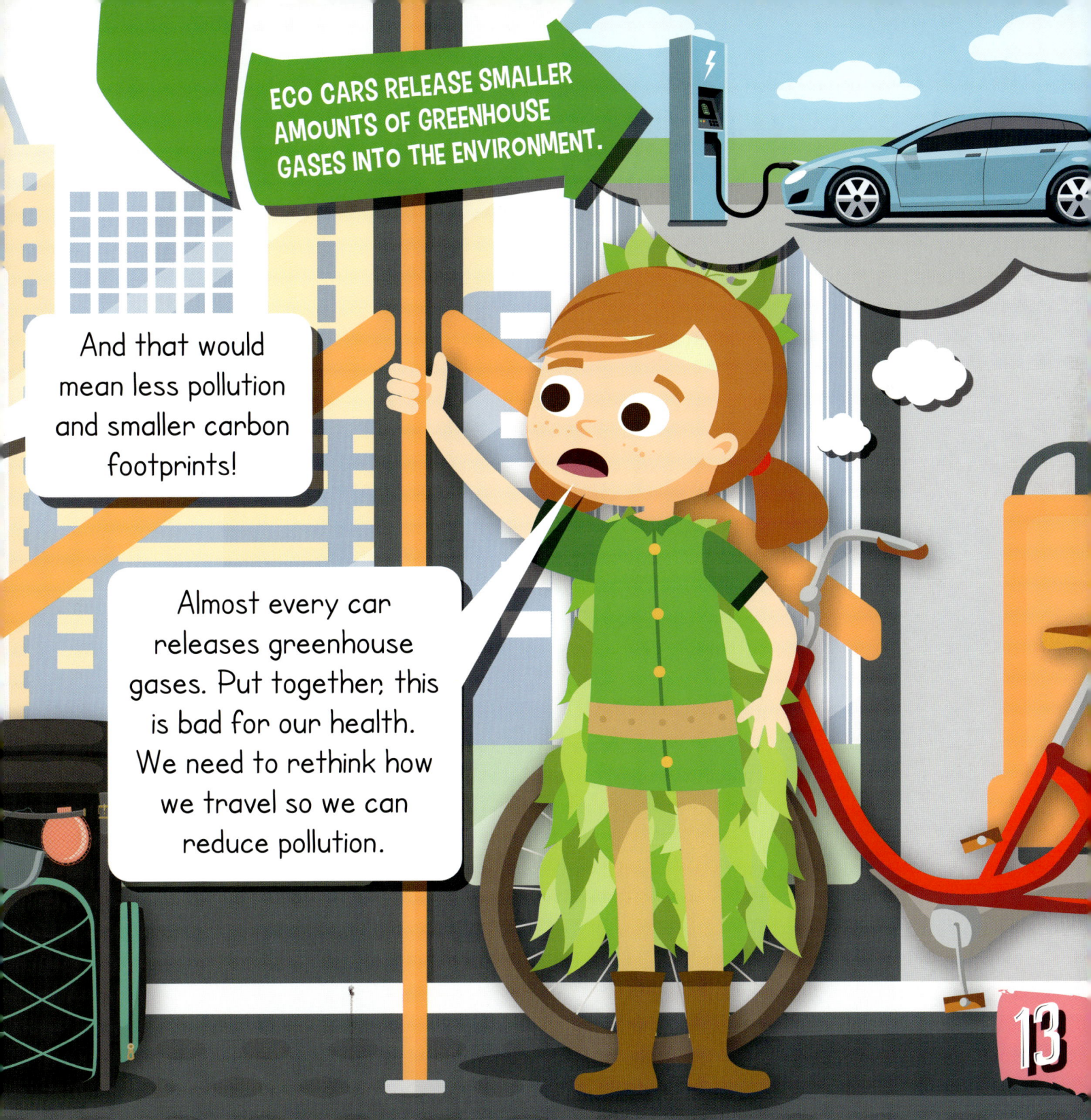

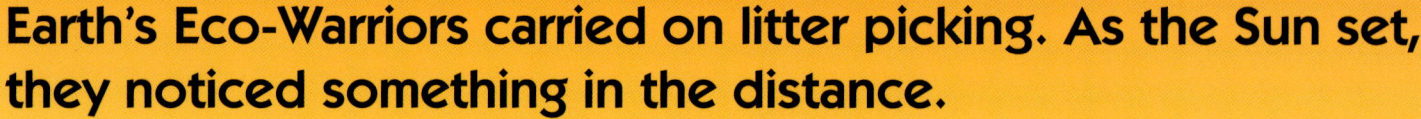

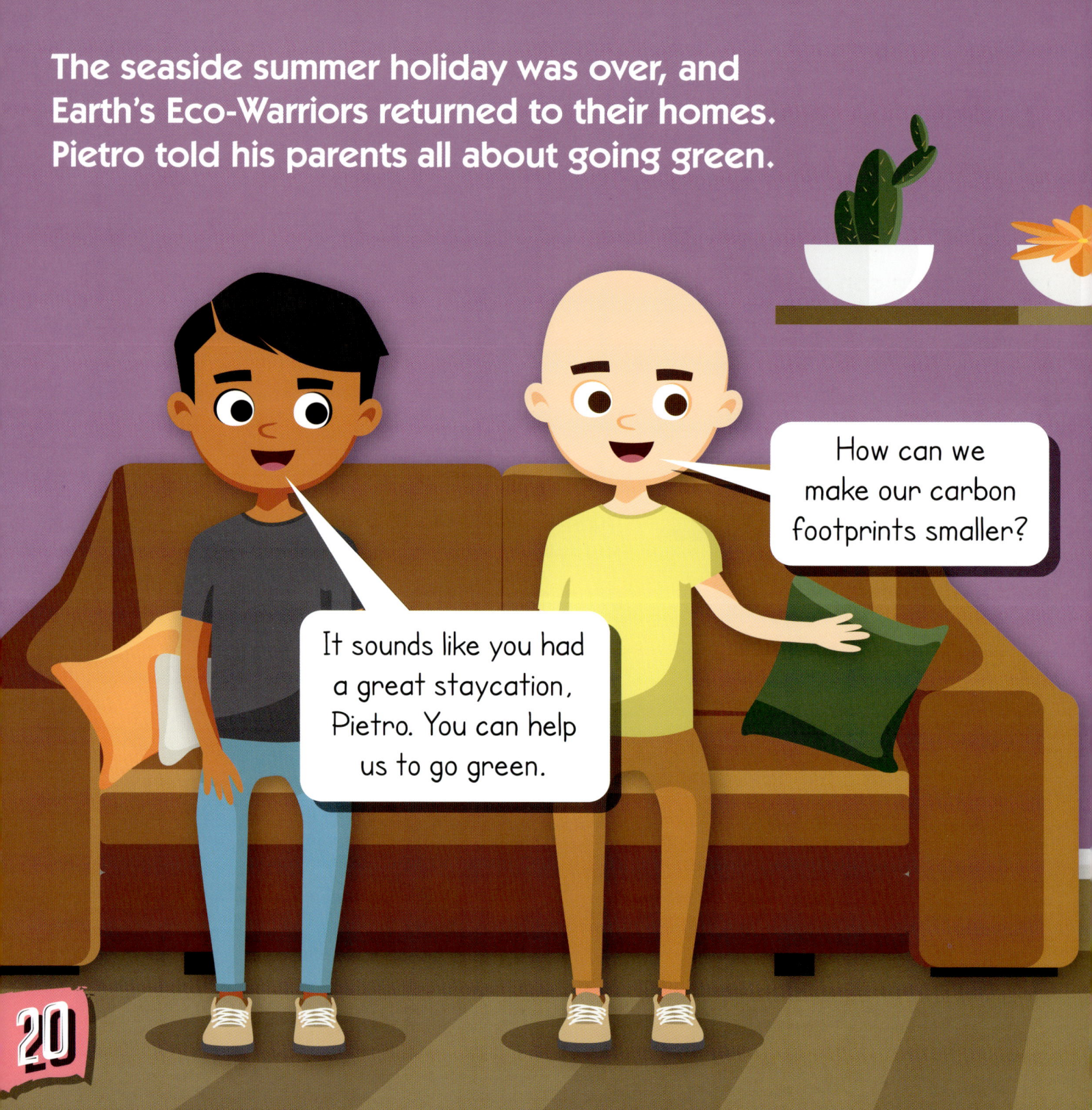

REDUCING CARBON FOOTPRINTS

The next day, Pietro showed his parents more ways to reduce their carbon footprints. He showed them a special website. People who are looking to make up for the size of their carbon footprints can visit the website and give money to projects all over the world.

THIS IS CALLED CARBON OFFSETTING.

Some projects plant trees around the world and other projects help people to rethink how they live. Would you like to find out more about carbon offsetting?

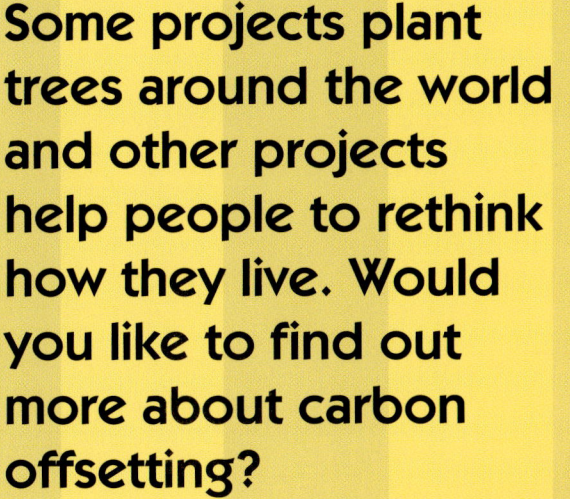

Visit this website to work out your carbon footprint:

https://footprint.wwf.org.uk/#/

Learn more about carbon offsetting on this website:

carbonfootprint.com/offsetshop.html

ECO-WORDS

atmosphere	the mixture of gases that make up the air and surround the Earth
carbon offsetting	making up for the size of your carbon footprint by giving money to projects that lower the amount of carbon in the atmosphere
compost bin	a special bin where garden waste and some food scraps such as vegetable peels turn into soil
crude oil	a liquid that is found underneath the ground and is used as a fuel
energy	a type of power, such as light or heat, that can be used to do something
environment	the natural world
fuel	something that can be used to make energy or power something
greenhouse gases	gases in the atmosphere that trap the Sun's heat
natural resources	useful materials that are created by nature
pollution	harmful and poisonous things being added to an environment
renewable	not able to run out
standby	a mode where something looks like it is turned off, but still uses energy
staycation	going on holiday close to home or in your home country
sustainable	to be done in a way that doesn't harm the environment or use up Earth's natural resources
turbines	machines that use flowing materials such as air or water to turn blades and make energy

INDEX

aeroplanes 5
animals 15, 17
bicycles 9, 11, 21
carbon dioxide 5–7, 12
carbon footprints 2, 6, 9, 11, 13, 19–20, 22–23
energy 10, 18–19, 21
litter 15, 18
oil 16–17
Planet Promise 2–3, 14
pollution 5, 13
turbines 18

PHOTO CREDITS

Cover & Throughout – Olga1818, Bukavik, Lorelyn Medina. 2&3 – GenerationClash, 4&5 – Igogosha, Bukavik, Tartila, 6&7 – piggu, Oliver Hoffmann, KittyVector, Inspiring, robuart, 8&9 – HappyPictures, Elvetica, 10&11 – CandyDuck, Anatolir, Sergey Mastepanov, Malinovskaya Yulia, intararit, 12&13 – Visual Generation, Kitty Vector, petovarga, 14&15 – aliaksei kruhlenia, the8monkey, 16&17 – Maquiadora, intararit, 20&21 – Diana Vasileva, 22&23 – Amanita Silvicora.

Images are courtesy of Shutterstock.com. With thanks to Getty Images, Thinkstock Photo and iStockphoto.

All facts, statistics, web addresses and URLs in this book were verified as valid and accurate at time of writing. No responsibility for any changes to external websites or references can be accepted by either the author or publisher.